How to Capture a Castle

Contents

Written by Rob Alcraft

Collins

How to capture a castle

This is going to be risky and difficult work. But if you have the money and time, any castle can be taken.

You will, of course, need a few things. You will need to use all kinds of weapons and sneakiness. You'll need many soldiers and **siege** experts, along with heaps of gold coins to pay for it all. You may also need a whale – but more about that later.

So, if you're ready, let's start with a few tips.

Bodiam Castle, England. Even a castle like this can be captured.

CASTLES RULE!

Safe inside with their soldiers and their treasure, a castle's owner could control all the land around, and tell everyone what to do. That was until someone took their castle from them.

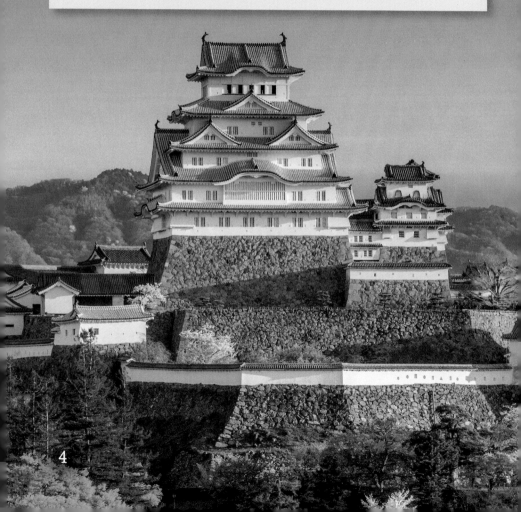

CASTLE CASE STUDY

Castles are built to keep you out. This is Himeji Castle in Japan. It is protected by giant stone walls, and water-filled **moats**.

If you do get inside, you'll find yourself in a maze of narrow passages, controlled by 84 gates. It will be easy to get lost, and hard to fight. To capture a castle like this will need skill and cunning – and a lot of soldiers.

CASTLE CASE STUDY

Monzón Castle, Spain. Powerful rulers built many thousands of stone and brick castles like this one around the world. They were all-powerful until the late 1600s, when **gunpowder** and reliable cannons made capturing a castle a bit easier. You just had to blow it to pieces!

1 Let the castle-capturing begin!

First, you must know the dangers. Let's have a closer look at what you're up against.

high towers

It's hard to surprise a castle. The castle's defenders will see you coming.

the keep

The **keep** is the heart of the castle, and hardest of all to break into.

loopholes

Expect deadly missiles like arrows and **musket** fire from these narrow slits.

cliffs and moats

Castles use cliffs and rivers to make them easier to defend. There are steep ditches and **embankments**, and sometimes a moat. It will be hard to even get close.

This picture gives you a good idea of what to expect. Everyone will be chucking things at you!

battlements

Watch the **battlements**. Be ready for rocks, **quicklime** and **crossbow bolts** to come flying at you.

thick walls

High stone walls like these can be as thick as a street. You will need to get over or under, or smash through them.

2 Beware of tricks and traps

You will need to take care. Castles are designed to be tricky.

It might be tempting to attack these gates – but this **barbican** will be well defended. There may be a drawbridge and **portcullis** gates that drop quickly. The idea is to trap you in a killing zone – so be careful.

the barbican

murder holes

These holes are placed in ceilings above gateways. The castle's defenders will use them to drop all kinds of deadly nastiness on top of you.

towers

Towers like these let defenders shoot in all directions. There'll be nowhere for you to hide from deadly arrows or musket balls. Towers may also have a base that spreads out, called a **talus**. Getting close to do proper damage will be difficult.

Watch out!

Look out for secret passages, hidden doorways and **posterns**. Defenders may use them to sneak up on you.

3 Gather your army

The first thing you're going to need to capture a castle is an army – a large one. You'll need all kinds of **knights** and soldiers, and siege experts too. Each one will have to be paid, making this one of the most expensive things you ever do!

CASTLE CASE STUDY

This picture shows an attack on Osaka Castle, Japan. In 1615, nearly 200,000 soldiers took part in fighting to take this castle. They had to fill in the outer moat so they could cross and finally capture it.

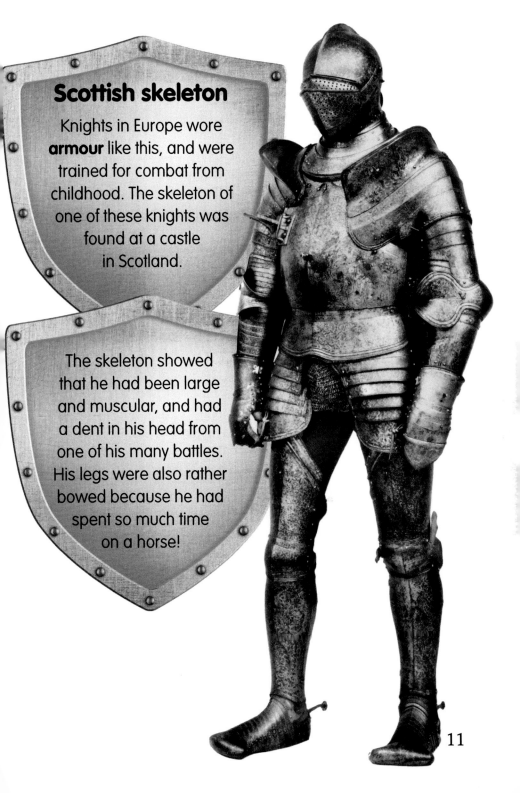

Scottish skeleton

Knights in Europe wore **armour** like this, and were trained for combat from childhood. The skeleton of one of these knights was found at a castle in Scotland.

The skeleton showed that he had been large and muscular, and had a dent in his head from one of his many battles. His legs were also rather bowed because he had spent so much time on a horse!

11

Your army must include archers. Their job will be to rain arrows down onto the castle, forcing defenders to take cover. Your soldiers can then attack walls and towers.

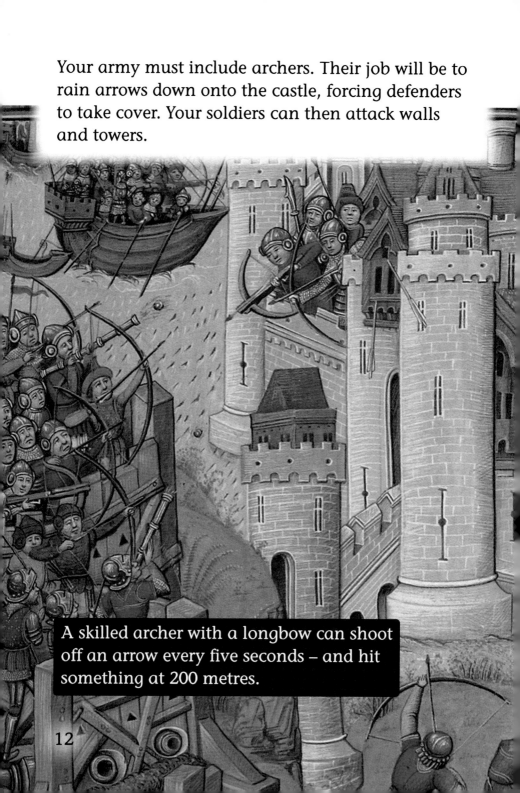

A skilled archer with a longbow can shoot off an arrow every five seconds – and hit something at 200 metres.

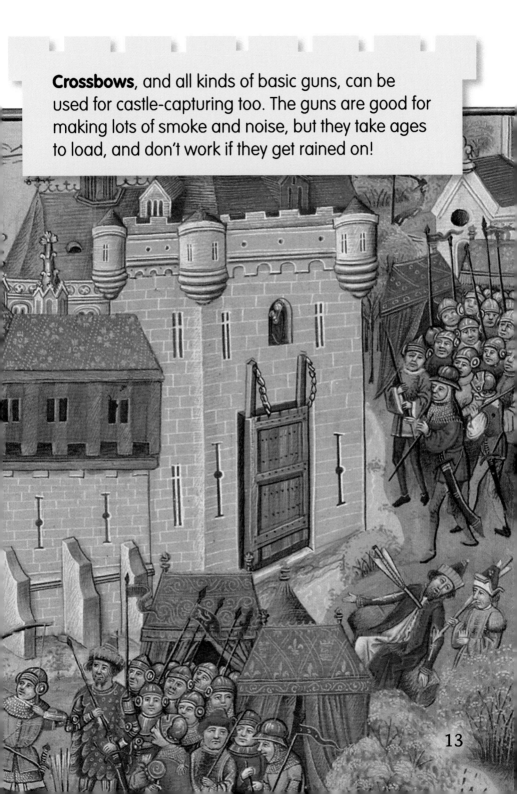

Crossbows, and all kinds of basic guns, can be used for castle-capturing too. The guns are good for making lots of smoke and noise, but they take ages to load, and don't work if they get rained on!

13

4 Stock up on supplies

Along with your army, you will need mountains of food for everyone to eat, and masses of castle-capturing equipment. To supply the army with food at one English siege, the Sheriff of London sent a whale! You may not be able to get hold of a whole whale – but make sure your army is well supplied.

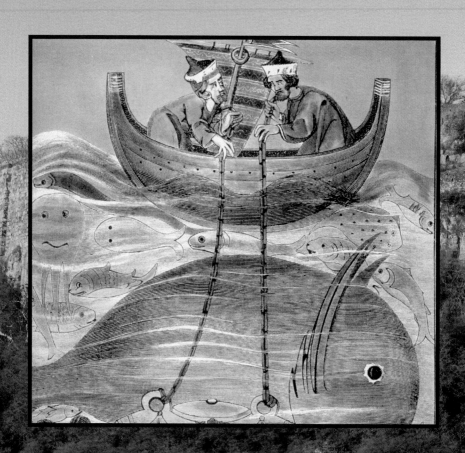

Make a shopping list

For his siege of Rochester Castle in England, records show that King John ordered up a massive list of things he needed. On the list was everything from rock-throwing catapults to ladders, shields and ropes – and two barrels full of coins.

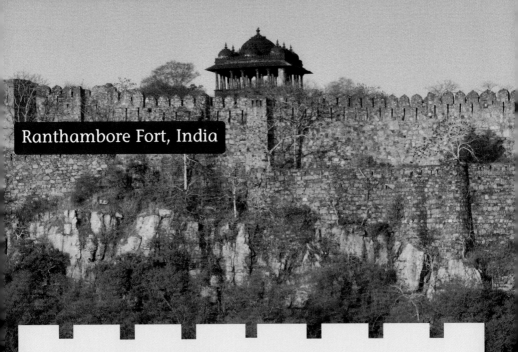

Ranthambore Fort, India

Don't forget shovels!

Capturing a castle can often involve a lot of digging. At Ranthambore Fort in India, attackers dug a huge mound higher than the fort itself. Then they rained rocks and arrows down onto the defenders and overwhelmed them.

15

5 Make a deal

Capturing a castle can sometimes cost more than building one. So avoid lots of nasty and expensive fighting: be smart, and make a deal. Negotiate with the castle's defenders, and give them a chance to hand over the castle peacefully.

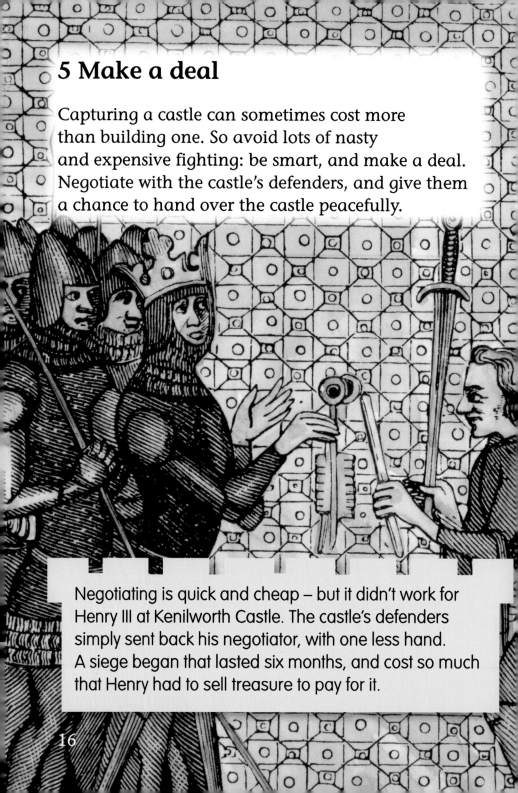

Negotiating is quick and cheap – but it didn't work for Henry III at Kenilworth Castle. The castle's defenders simply sent back his negotiator, with one less hand. A siege began that lasted six months, and cost so much that Henry had to sell treasure to pay for it.

CASTLE CASE STUDY

It doesn't have to end badly ...

At the siege of Weinsberg, Germany, in 1140, a deal was made before any fighting and nastiness began. The men would have to stay, but all the women could go free, with whatever they could carry. So the women left the castle – carrying their men with them!

6 Surround the enemy

If negotiating won't work, you must begin your siege. Surround the castle, and stop any supplies of food and weapons getting in. If you can wait long enough, the defenders will run out of food and be forced to surrender. The castle will be yours.

You should look scary and be loud. The more worried the castle's defenders feel, the more they will want to surrender. Bang drums and shields, and shout your favourite insults!

CASTLE CASE STUDY

Harlech Castle in Wales could be supplied from the sea through a **fortified** stairway. This made it very difficult to stop fresh supplies of food and weapons getting in. It once held out against seven years of attacks, and it eventually took an army of 10,000 to capture it.

7 Build defences

Remember that the castle you're surrounding is full of armed soldiers. They may come out at any moment and attack *you*. Build defences – think mini-castle! You'll need ditches, an embankment and a **stockade** of wooden posts to keep you safe.

CASTLE CASE STUDY

Don't get caught by surprise. At Pontefract Castle, England, castle defenders used a hidden door to make surprise attacks, and capture supplies. They even managed to bring a herd of cows back with them into the castle. If you let food and other goodies get through your siege, it will drag on for months.

Expect injury!

This is a ballista – a giant crossbow used by castle defenders. It fires heavy iron-tipped bolts. One man was hit head-on by one of these and, rather surprisingly, survived to write about it later.

8 Be sneaky!

When it comes to castle-capturing, sneakiness can be very useful. You have several sneaky options that have worked in the past.

CASTLE CASE STUDY

Can you fake a letter? The massive Krak des Chevaliers castle, in what is now Syria, could hold up to 2,000 soldiers, but it fell to attackers – easy-peasy. The attackers sent in a forged letter, pretending to be from the defenders' commander. The letter told them to surrender – and they did!

Krak des Chevaliers, Syria

CASTLE CASE STUDY

Like dressing up? Disguise can be a winning bit of sneakiness! With disguise, it took just 13 soldiers to capture one English castle. All they did was to turn up dressed as local delivery men. The gates were opened – and in they went.

Moo!

Roxburgh Castle in Scotland was captured in 1313 by soldiers who crept up on it disguised as cows. What could you try?

Any castle will fall to the right sneaky **tactic** – even the massive Castle Gaillard. But you mustn't be afraid to get a little dirty.

In 1204, the castle had held out for six months before attackers smashed through an outer wall. Still the defenders fought on, so it was time to get sneaky.

Castle Gaillard, France.
Built in 1198, it was ringed by
two sets of walls and towers.

Looking for a way into the heart of the castle, the attackers found an unguarded toilet drain that led up into the castle's chapel. It was roomy enough to get inside – so in they went.

No one was expecting armed soldiers to crawl out of their toilet, so the attackers made it inside. They opened the gates, let their soldiers in and took the castle. Sneakiness wins again!

9 Use bribes

A long castle siege will get a bit miserable – so speed things up and use cash **bribes** if you can.

CASTLE CASE STUDY

This is the fortress at Golconda, India. Built high on a rocky hill, it had five kilometres of walls and high-powered cannons, but these couldn't protect it against sneakiness. It was captured in 1687 when someone was bribed to open a gate.

CASTLE CASE STUDY

Bribes worked well at Threave Castle in Scotland. Attackers spent three months trying to smash their way inside, before deciding that a bribe might be easier. It was! The castle's commander accepted five pounds, 13 shillings and six pence to hand over the building.

Threave Castle, Scotland

Fancy a biscuit?

One castle was captured in 1341 with a simple offer of treats and biscuits for the gatekeeper. He opened the gates to get his biscuits, and soldiers rushed in and took the castle!

27

10 Attack the walls

Some castles will have enough food and water to hold out for months. Waiting about will be costly, so you need to speed things up and find a way to get past the castle walls.

A siege tower has to be taller than the castle walls.

One way over a castle's walls is to use siege towers. Think big. At a castle siege in 1266, three huge siege towers were used, one so enormous it could hold 200 archers.

Ladders let soldiers climb in safely.

With wheels, the tower can be moved up to the castle walls – but if there's a moat, you will have to fill it in. Use those shovels to start moving earth and rubble.

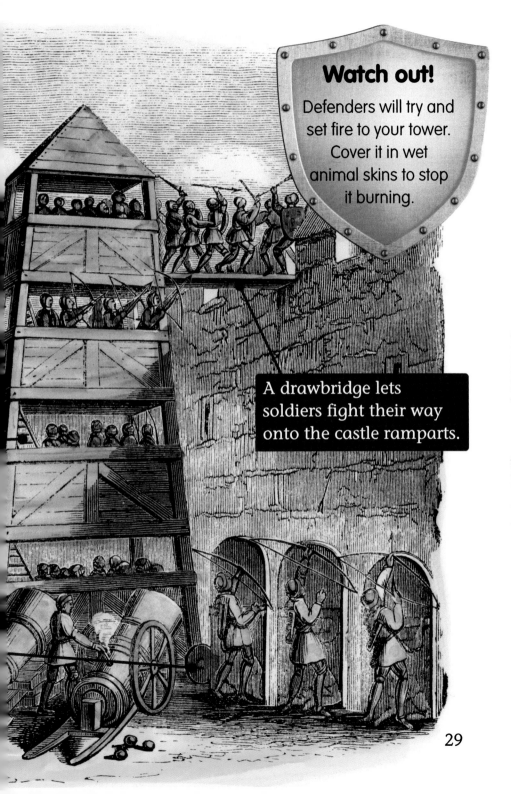

Watch out!

Defenders will try and set fire to your tower. Cover it in wet animal skins to stop it burning.

A drawbridge lets soldiers fight their way onto the castle ramparts.

Another speedy way into a castle is to use ladders or ropes, and climb the walls. It's quick, but dangerous! But if you can't get over the castle walls, then digging might be the answer. Making tunnels can collapse castle walls, and give you a chance to get inside.

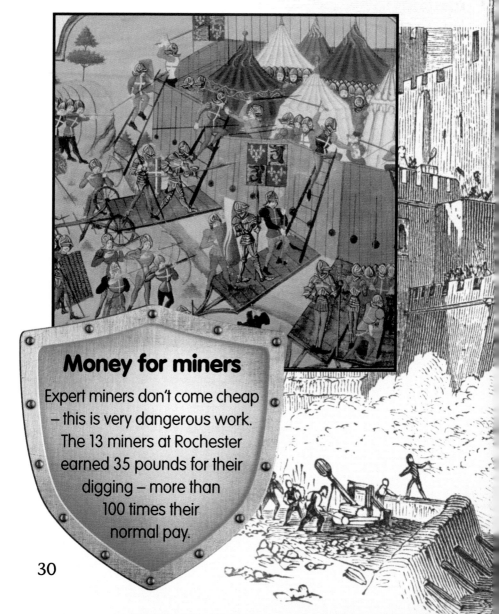

Money for miners

Expert miners don't come cheap – this is very dangerous work. The 13 miners at Rochester earned 35 pounds for their digging – more than 100 times their normal pay.

CASTLE CASE STUDY

Digging works wonders.
At the siege of Rochester Castle in 1215, miners worked for more than six weeks, digging tunnels underneath the castle walls. They then collapsed the tunnels, bringing down half of Rochester's massive keep – and the castle was taken.

Takamatsu Castle in Japan –
defeated by digging and water.

A good bit of digging can properly wreck the chances
of even the strongest castle. Just be prepared for some
hard work!

In 1582, Takamatsu Castle held out against 20,000
soldiers. It stood in the middle of a marsh, making it
impossible to get heavy siege towers or anything else
close enough to do proper damage. So the attackers
came up with a plan – and began digging.

In 12 days, they built a dam across a nearby river, and a series of dykes and channels four kilometres long, to divert the water towards the castle.
The marshy land around the castle became a lake – allowing the attackers to use boats, and finally get close enough to force the castle's surrender.

11 Smash your way in!

Sometimes the only way into a castle is to smash through the walls or gates. You have several very destructive options.

Battering rams can smash open a castle's gates – and so can an elephant. Elephants were a favourite battle weapon for castle-capturing in India.

This is a giant catapult – called a trebuchet. It can fling huge rock balls over 300 metres, and give castle walls a good pounding. And you don't have to limit yourself to rocks. Fire balls can set light to a castle's insides, and dead animals and manure are favourites to throw over castle walls to try and spread disease.

Giant weapons

Giant catapults were often given tough-sounding names. One of the biggest was known as Warwolf, and another was called Buster!

Another way to properly smash up a castle is with gunpowder and cannons. You'll be able to do lots of lovely damage, but be warned, this is very unstable technology.

CASTLE CASE STUDY

Be a bit careful

The Scottish king, James II, was good at capturing castles – and liked to use cannons to get the job done. But, as it turned out, James was a little *too* fond of his cannons. At his last siege in 1460, he was showing off one of his favourites when it blew apart – taking him with it.

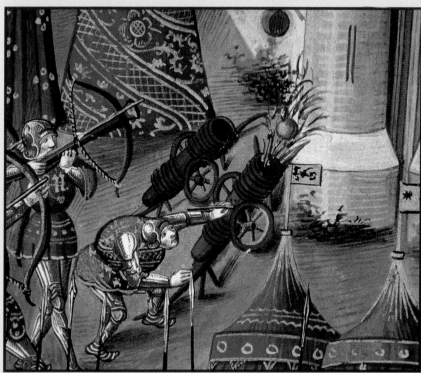

This a petard, a kind of bomb that will blow open a castle's gates. It can be useful in a siege – but may blow you up too!

This is Goodrich Castle in England. By the time it faced its last siege in 1646, gunpowder and cannons were a bit more reliable.

The siege had dragged on for so long that its defenders had run out of supplies and weapons, and were left throwing rocks from the battlements. Meanwhile, the attackers had had time to order up a brand-new cannon.

Given the name Roaring Meg, the cannon fired giant balls filled with gunpowder. Steadily, Roaring Meg began to blow the castle apart. By the time the defenders surrendered, there wasn't a single room in the castle left whole.

This is Roaring Meg – a special kind of cannon called a bombard, and just what's needed for blowing apart a castle.

12 Claim your victory

By now, you should have made some kind of hole in the castle or got ladders and siege towers in place. Attack now, and all the loot in the castle will soon be yours.

Turn captives into cash!

England's King John made sure that being on the losing side would cost you. He had **scrolls** full of the fines and **ransoms** he was owed. From one captive, he demanded three warhorses and six suits of armour. Another man was fined about the price of a whole new castle – and ordered to hand over his grandchildren to make sure he paid up.

CASTLE CASE STUDY

When the Red Fort in India was captured, it held fabulous treasures, including several of the largest diamonds in the world. England's Tower of London had a zoo inside it, with a polar bear, a leopard and an elephant. What will you find inside your captured castle?

You are the king of the castle

Now you have your very own castle! But keeping it might be difficult. As you know by now, you'll need heaps of gold coins and a lot of soldiers. And after all the smashing up you've just done, you will also need to do some rebuilding. Then someone will try and take the castle from *you*.

Edinburgh Castle in Scotland was attacked and **besieged** 23 times – and changed hands nearly as often. You might not be king of your castle for very long.

Edinburgh Castle, Scotland

Glossary

armour layers of metal and leather used for protection

barbican a gate tower

battlements walkways on a castle's walls

besieged surrounded and attacked a castle by cutting off supplies

bribes give someone money to get them to do what you want

crossbow bolts heavy, thick arrows

crossbows weapons that shoot arrows

embankments walls of heaped earth

fortified protected by strong walls and towers

gunpowder explosive powder

keep a high tower in the middle of a castle

knights soldiers who often fought on horseback

loopholes slits in a wall for shooting through

moats protective ditches, sometimes filled with water

musket an early kind of gun

portcullis a heavy gate made of criss-crossed wood

posterns small hidden gates

quicklime powder which burns the skin

ransoms money demanded for releasing a captive

scrolls rolls of paper for writing on

siege surrounding and attacking a castle by cutting off supplies

stockade a wall of wooden posts

tactic a way of doing something

talus a thick, sloping base on a castle wall

Index

Can you capture this castle?

What will you use first?

attack forces

bribery

weapons

siege engines

food and supplies

gunpowder

climbing

negotiating

mining

Ideas for reading

Written by Christine Whitney
Primary Literacy Consultant

Reading objectives:
- be introduced to non-fiction books that are structured in different ways
- listen to, discuss and express views about non-fiction
- retrieve and record information from non-fiction
- discuss and clarify the meanings of words

Spoken language objectives:
- participate in discussion
- speculate, hypothesise, imagine and explore ideas through talk
- ask relevant questions

Curriculum links: History: Develop an awareness of the past; Writing: Write for different purposes

Word count: 3087

Interest words: siege, besiege, negotiate, tactics, fortified

Resources: paper, pencils and crayons, access to the internet, recyclable materials or building bricks for building a model castle

Build a context for reading

- Ask children if they have ever visited a castle. Ask the group to name as many facts about castles as they can in five minutes.
- Show the book cover to them and read the title, *How to Capture a Castle*. Ask for a volunteer to explain why someone might want *to capture a castle*.
- Read the blurb on the back cover. Ask children what they understand by the word *lessons* – with **lessons** *from 700 years of history*.
- Challenge the group to suggest three *tactics* that might be used to capture a castle. Check understanding of the word *tactics*.

Understand and apply reading strategies

- Turn to the contents page and read through the chapter titles. Ask children to say which chapter they most want to read and why.
- Read together up to the end of Chapter 1. Support children as they list the dangers of castle-capturing!